My First Bible in Pictu

T0022791

by

....

on

....

KENNETH N. TAYLOR

My First
Bible
IN PICTURES

with illustrations by Richard and Frances Hook

Tyndale House Publishers
Carol Stream, Illinois

Visit Tyndale's website for kids at tyndale.com/kids.

TYNDALE is a registered trademark of Tyndale House Ministries. The Tyndale Kids logo is a trademark of Tyndale House Ministries.

My First Bible in Pictures: 30th Anniversary Edition

Designed by Jacqueline L. Nuñez

This book contains more than 100 beautiful illustrations by Richard and Frances Hook. Tyndale House gratefully acknowledges the following publishers for permission to print their Hook art:

Concordia Publishing House: The Hook illustrations on pages 41, 133, 155, 167, 185, 189, 203, 221, 231, and 233 are taken from *My Good Shepherd Bible Story Book*, copyright 1969 by Concordia Publishing House, St. Louis, MO 63118, and are used by permission.

The Standard Publishing Company: The Hook illustrations on pages 75 and 243 are taken from *Frances Hook Picture Book*, copyright 1963, 1964 by The Standard Publishing Company, Cincinnati, OH 45231, and are used by permission.

Other artists:

Ron Ferris: pages 5, 9, 13, 17, 25, 93, 107, 113, 119, 125, 153, 219, 251.

Corbert Gauthier: pages 35, 39, 55, 57, 67, 87, 89, 103, 115, 139, 201.

Janice Skivington Wood: page 253.

For manufacturing information regarding this product, please call 1-855-277-9400.

For information about special discounts for bulk purchases, please contact Tyndale House Ministries at csresponse@tyndale.com, or call 1-855-277-9400.

Library of Congress Cataloging-in-Publication Data

A catalog record for this book is available from the Library of Congress.

ISBN 978-1-4964-5123-1

Printed in China

28	27	26	25	24	23	22
7	6	5	4	3	2	1

A Note to Parents

This is a "carry-to-church" book of Bible stories for little people. But don't leave it on the shelf during the week. Read it with your children at home. The stories and illustrations introduce children to the great people of the Bible. The important themes of the Bible will be planted in little lives, to grow there throughout a lifetime. Above all, the stories tell about God and his Son, Jesus, and about God's demand for truth and righteousness.

Many of the stories have obvious applications for young children. A simple question brings home the truth of each story, helping to anchor important facts in children's minds.

For many, many years I have been writing to help children grow in the grace of God. I hope this book, doubtless one of my final efforts, will accomplish its purpose in your children's lives. May God bless each one of them in a special way.

Kenneth N. Taylor

GOD MADE

the whole world. He made the flowers and the trees and the water and the stars. God made the sun so we can have daylight. The sun makes us warm when we are outside on sunny days. Thank you, God, for making the sun.

Who made the sun?

ADAM AND EVE

were the very first man and woman.
God made them. He gave them
a beautiful place to live called the
Garden of Eden. They were very
happy. God made the animals, too.
Point to the elephant. Where is
the zebra?

Who made Adam and Eve?

ADAM AND EVE

are sorry and sad. They did something God told them not to do. Now God is punishing them. They must go away from their nice home in the Garden of Eden. The angels won't let them go back.

Why must Adam and Eve leave their nice home?

ADAM AND EVE

had two sons. Their names are
Cain and Abel. Abel obeyed God,
but Cain did not obey God. Cain
was angry and killed Abel. This was
wrong. Adam and Eve were very
sad. God was sad too.

*What are the names of Adam
and Eve's sons?*

GOD TOLD NOAH

to build a huge boat. It is called an
ark. Noah's sons are helping him.
The ark is not in the water. But
soon it will begin to rain and rain
until there is water everywhere.
Noah and all his family will
be safe in the boat.

*Where will Noah and his family
be when it rains?*

NOAH FINISHED

building the boat. Then God told
him to bring two of each kind
of animal and bird into the boat.
There are two giraffes and two
tigers and two ducks. They will all
be safe in the ark when
the flood comes.

How many kangaroos are there?

IT RAINED

and rained and rained.
Soon everything was covered
with water. But Noah's boat is
floating on the water. Yes, God
took care of Noah and his family
and the animals in the boat.
God takes care of you, too.

Who is in the boat?

THE PEOPLE

are building a big tower.

It is called the Tower of Babel.

The people think they can build

it up to heaven. But God doesn't

want them to build the tower.

He will make them stop.

Suddenly they won't understand

each other's words!

*Who made the people stop building
the tower?*

ABRAHAM WAS

a special friend of God. His wife
is Sarah. God told Abraham to
move to another country. God said
he would give Abraham the entire
country for his family to live in
forever. Abraham has many sheep
and donkeys. Can you point
to them?

*What is the man's name? What is his
wife's name?*

ABRAHAM

and his wife, Sarah, were very sad because they didn't have any children. But who is this big boy? Now they have a son. His name is Isaac. They are happy because God answered their prayer and gave them a son.

What is the name of Abraham and Sarah's son?

WHEN ISAAC

grew up, he married Rebekah
and had a son named Jacob. Jacob
was tired and went to sleep with his
head on a rock for a pillow! He had
a dream about angels going up and
down from heaven. Then God told
Jacob, "I will take care of you."

What did Jacob dream about?

JACOB HAD A TWIN

brother named Esau. When the
boys grew up, they had a big
argument. Jacob moved far away.
Finally he sent a message to Esau.
He said he hoped they could be
friends again. Now they are happy
to see each other.

What are the names of the brothers?

THE OLD MAN

is Jacob. He has twelve sons. He
loves his son Joseph very much.
He gave Joseph a beautiful coat.
Joseph's brothers are angry
because their father didn't give
them nice coats too. They should be
happy for Joseph.

What did Joseph's father give him?

THIS BABY'S NAME

is Moses. The young woman is
a princess. She found the baby
in a basket in a river. Bad men
wanted to kill the baby. God sent
the princess to find the baby Moses
and take care of him.

*Where did the princess find
the baby Moses?*

NOW MOSES

has become a big man. One day he saw a bush on fire, but it didn't burn up! God spoke to Moses from the bush. God said, "Go and help my people." Moses was afraid at first, but God said, "I will help you."

What did God tell Moses to do?

GOD'S PEOPLE

are living in Egypt. The man with
the whip is telling them to work
harder. They will ask God to help
them. God will send Moses to make
the man stop hurting them. Moses
will help all of God's people.

Who will help God's people?

MOSES TOLD

Pharaoh to let God's people
move away from Egypt. Pharaoh
said no. God sent many flies and
frogs and other problems to bother
the Egyptians. Pharaoh still said no.
Finally God said he would kill the
oldest boy in each family in Egypt.

What did Moses tell Pharaoh?

MOSES TOLD

God's people to put blood above
their doors and beside their doors.
God would not kill anyone in the
house if he saw blood at the door.
The night this happened is called
the Passover. Finally Pharaoh said
God's people could leave Egypt.
They left that night.

Why is there blood above the door?

EXODUS 14

GOD'S PEOPLE

are walking along the bottom of
a big lake called the Red Sea. Can
you see the water standing up along
both sides? When Moses held up
his stick, God made the water open
up. Now the people can walk on dry
ground through the lake.

Who made the water open up?

38

THIS FAMILY

is picking up little pieces of bread. God sent the bread down from heaven so his people would not be hungry. God fed his people this way every morning. Point to the little girl who is saying thank you to God.

Where did the bread come from?

GOD'S PEOPLE

were very thirsty, but they didn't have anything to drink. God told Moses to hit the rock with his stick. When he did this, God made water come out of the rock. Then everyone could have a big drink.

What happened when Moses hit the rock with his stick?

MOSES IS LISTENING

to God. God is telling Moses
ten very important rules he wants
his people to obey. God wrote
these ten rules on pieces of stone.
These rules are called the Ten
Commandments.

What are God's ten rules called?

OH, NO!

See what God's people are doing!
They made an idol that looks like a
calf. They are worshiping the idol
instead of worshiping God. This
made God angry and sad. God had
to punish them for doing this.

What are these people doing?
Why is this bad?

THIS BEAUTIFUL

tent is called the Tabernacle.
It was God's house. People came
here to say thank you to God
and to pray to him. The people
worshiped God in the Tabernacle. It
was their church.

*Does the Tabernacle look
like your church?*

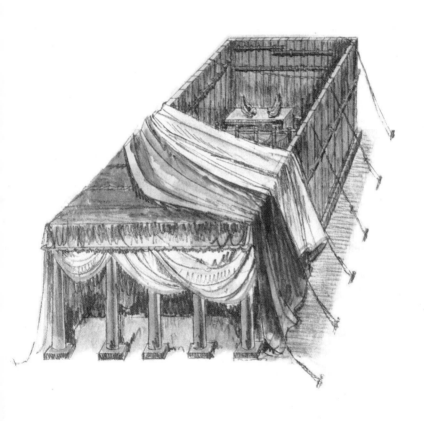

MOSES IS LEADING

the people on a long trip.
How does Moses know where to
go? He is looking up to watch a
special cloud that God put there.
Moses and the people follow
wherever God moves the cloud.
Can you point to the cloud?

Who is moving the cloud?

LOOK AT THE BIG

bunch of grapes these men
are carrying! The men's names
are Caleb and Joshua. The grapes
grew in the country God promised
to give to his people. The men
are hurrying home to show their
friends what good things grow in
the Promised Land.

Where did these grapes grow?

SNAKES WERE

biting God's people, and some
of the people died. God told Moses
to make something that looked like
a big snake. The people who were
bitten could look up at the snake
on the pole. Then God made
them well again.

Who made the people well again?

GOD DIDN'T WANT

Balaam to go down this road.
So God sent an angel to stop him.
When the donkey saw the angel,
it stopped. Balaam hit the donkey
to make it go again. Then the
donkey talked! It asked, "Why did
you hit me?" Finally Balaam saw
the angel and was glad the
donkey stopped!

What did the donkey say?

JOSHUA WAS

the next leader of God's people. God told him to destroy the town of Jericho. Joshua and all the people walked around the walls and blew their trumpets and shouted. Now all the walls are falling down so God's people can go in.

What is happening to the walls?

GIDEON WANTED

to take ten thousand soldiers with him to fight God's enemies. God wanted him to take only a few. God told Gideon to choose only the three hundred men who drank from their hands. Gideon was afraid to have such a small army, but God said he would help him.

How many soldiers did Gideon take?

SAMSON WAS

a very, very strong man. See how easily he broke the ropes! Once he killed a lion with his bare hands. Another time he knocked down a palace to punish God's enemies. God made him strong so he could help God's people.

What is the man's name?

JOB 1

THE MAN

in the white robe is Job
(his name rhymes with *robe*).
He was a good man who always
tried to do what God said. Then
Satan asked God to let terrible
things happen to Job. Job was very
sad, but he still loved God.

Did Job always love God?

THE LADY IN BLUE

is Naomi. She is sad because her husband and sons have died. Ruth is trying to help Naomi feel better. She will stay with Naomi. God wants us to be helpers too. What can you do to help someone?

What is the name of the woman who is helping Naomi?

SAMUEL WAS ONLY

a little boy, but he lived at the Tabernacle and helped Eli the priest. One night he heard a voice calling his name. At first he thought it was Eli. But it was God's voice. God had a message for Samuel. Samuel listened to God and obeyed.

Who was calling Samuel?

AFTER SAMUEL

grew up, God's people wanted a
king. God was not happy about this.
He knew there would be problems.
But he chose Saul to be the king.
Saul was tall and handsome.
Samuel tells the people, "Here is
your new king. Obey him."

Who became the king?

DAVID WAS

a special friend of God. When
he was a boy he took care of his
father's sheep. Can you see his harp
beside him? He wrote beautiful
songs to tell God that he loved him.
Many of his songs are in the Bible.
They are called the Psalms.

What did David write?

THIS LION

wants to eat David's sheep.
Can you point to the lion?
Where are the sheep? God has
made David strong and brave.
With God's help David will kill
the lion so it can't hurt
the sheep.

Will the lion hurt the sheep?
Why not?

GOLIATH WANTS

to hurt God's people with his spear and sword. David is using his slingshot to throw a stone at Goliath. David knows God will help him. The stone will hit Goliath on his face and Goliath will fall down, dead. God's people will be safe.

Who killed Goliath?

KING SAUL

had a son named Jonathan. David and Jonathan were best friends. But King Saul wanted to kill David. Jonathan helped David hide from the king. Jonathan knew he must obey God and help David even if his father said he should not do this. You and I must always obey God too.

Who was David's friend?

IT IS NIGHT,

and King Saul is asleep. He has been trying to find David to kill him. David has been hiding, but now he sees King Saul. Should David hurt the king? God does not want him to hurt King Saul. David will obey God.

Did David hurt the king?

SAMUEL IS OLD NOW,

but he is still one of God's helpers. God told him to pour olive oil on David's head. This is how God showed everyone that David would become the next king of God's people. God will help David be a good king.

Who would be the new king of God's people?

NOW DAVID

is the king of Israel. The big
golden box behind him is called
the Ark of the Covenant. He is
bringing the Ark to Jerusalem.
He is jumping for joy. He loves God
and God loves him. God loves you,
too. You should be very happy.

Why is King David so happy?

THIS BEAUTIFUL

woman is Bathsheba. King David
did something very wrong. He
killed Bathsheba's husband so he
could marry her. When he did this,
David broke some of God's most
important rules. This made God
very angry, so he punished David.

Why was God angry with David?

THIS IS

King David's son Absalom.
The king's soldiers were chasing
him because he did not obey the
king. Absalom was riding on his
donkey under the tree. His hair
got caught in the branches, and
his donkey left him hanging there.
Then King David's army found him.

What happened to Absalom's hair?

DAVID HAS

another son named Solomon.
God's helper, Nathan, is putting
his hands on Solomon's head
to make him the next king.
Solomon asked God to make him
a wise king. God was pleased with
Solomon and gave him
great wisdom.

*What did Solomon ask God
to give him?*

THESE TWO WOMEN

are fighting over the baby.
Each says the baby is hers.
God made King Solomon know
which woman was really the baby's
mother. He gave the baby back
to its mother. Then everyone
thanked God for giving them
such a wise king.

Why were the women arguing?

KING SOLOMON

built a beautiful church for God
called the Temple. Can you see him
standing there? He is thanking God.
The king is very happy because he
is God's helper. You and I can be
God's helpers too. This will make
God happy.

What did King Solomon build?

KING SOLOMON

is breaking one of God's most important rules. Do you know what he is doing wrong? He is praying to these animals made of gold. We know he should pray only to God. God is angry with him and will send many troubles into Solomon's life.

What did Solomon do wrong?

ELIJAH IS GOD'S

helper. He is called a prophet.
Elijah is very hungry. He loves God,
so God sent these birds to bring
him food. Can you see the bread
the birds are bringing him? God is
taking care of him. God takes care
of you, too.

What did the birds bring to Elijah?

ELIJAH ASKED GOD

to send fire from heaven. Can you
point to Elijah? He has his hands
lifted to God. Elijah is showing
that God is very powerful. Did God
answer Elijah's prayer? Yes!
Look at the fire God sent!

What did God send from heaven?

WHAT IS HAPPENING

here? God has sent horses made
of fire and a chariot made of fire to
take Elijah up to heaven!
No one has seen Elijah again.
He is in heaven with God. Elisha
will be the new prophet.

What are the horses made of?
Where did God take Elijah?

THE ONLY FOOD

this lady had was some olive oil
in a jar. God's new helper, Elisha,
told her to pour her oil into many
other jars. She poured and poured,
but her jar didn't get empty! Now
she can sell the jars of olive oil
and buy food.

How did Elisha help the woman?

THIS LADY

is Elisha's friend. One day
her little boy became ill and died.
The mother ran to Elisha and asked
him to help. Elisha prayed, and
the boy came back to life!
The boy's parents were glad.
God can do anything!

What happened to the boy?

THE MAN

in the chariot is sick. The little girl
told him that God's helper, Elisha,
could make him well. Naaman is
going away in his chariot to visit
Elisha. When Elisha prayed,
God made Naaman well.

What did the girl tell the sick man?

CAN YOU SEE

the tree on the ground? These young men were chopping it with axes. One man's axe fell into the river, and it sank to the bottom. But Elisha, God's helper, told the axe to float. Now the man can have it again.

What happened to the man's axe?

THESE PEOPLE

are happy. They are singing and playing on horns and drums as they walk to their church. They are telling God, "Thank you for helping us." You and I can thank God too. We can bow our heads and close our eyes and say, "Thank you, God."

What are these people telling God?

WHEN PRINCE JOASH

was a baby, his wicked grandmother wanted to kill him! His uncle and aunt hid Joash until he was seven. Now he has become king! The soldiers are taking his grandmother away so she can't hurt him. Joash loves God and is a good king.

How old is Joash?

THESE PEOPLE

are repairing their church building.
King Joash knows this is the right
thing to do. The people want to
have a place where everyone
can thank God for all the kind
things he does for them.

What would you like to thank God for?

JONAH DIDN'T

want to obey God. He tried to
run away on a boat, but God sent
a storm. Jonah was thrown into
the water. The big fish swallowed
him. After three days the fish
spit Jonah out onto the sand.
Now Jonah will obey God.

What happened to Jonah?

KING AHAZ

is a bad king. He is telling
the men to nail the church doors
shut. He doesn't want anyone
to go in and pray to God. God
will punish him for doing this.
Aren't you glad that no one has
nailed your church doors shut?

*What is happening to
the church doors?*

MANY OF THE KINGS

of God's people worshiped idols.
They taught God's people to pray
to idols. They asked the idols to
make their gardens grow.
They thanked the idols for rain.
This was foolish. Now King
Hezekiah's men are smashing the
idols and will only pray to God.

What are the men breaking?

THIS MAN

is reading God's rules to King Josiah. The king didn't know about these rules. Now he will obey them and do what God wants. We have God's rules in the Bible. When we read the Bible we can obey God and make him happy.

Where can we find God's rules?

JEREMIAH WAS ONE

of God's helpers. He told the people what God wanted them to do. Some men didn't want to listen, so they put him in this deep hole. Jeremiah was brave. When they took him out, he kept on telling them what God wanted them to do.

What is this man's name?

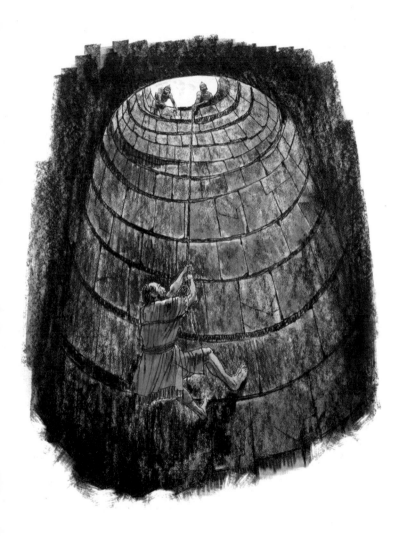

THE BEAUTIFUL

city of Jerusalem is burning.
The enemies of God's people have
set it on fire. Why did God let them
do this? It is because the people
in the city prayed to idols instead
of praying to God.

*What is happening to
the beautiful city?*

DANIEL AND HIS

three friends are talking to the king. The king burned the city of Jerusalem where they lived. But now the king likes Daniel and his friends. The king will ask them to help him rule the kingdom.

What will the king ask Daniel and his friends to do?

THE KING MADE

a big statue of himself and said
everyone must pray to it. But
Shadrach, Meshach, and Abednego
will not pray to the statue. They will
pray only to God. The king is angry
and says he will punish them.
But look in the next picture
to see what happened!

Why are these men standing up?

THE KING THREW

Shadrach, Meshach, and Abednego into the fire because they would pray only to God. But look! There are four men in the fire! God has sent his angel to take care of them! The fire didn't hurt them at all!

Who is taking care of them in the fire?

THE KING

is frightened. He sees a big hand.
The hand is writing on the wall.
The king can't read the words,
but God tells Daniel what the words
mean. The words say the king
has been bad. God will not let
him be king anymore.

What do the words on the wall say?

DANIEL PRAYED

only to God. He would not pray
to the king. The king's helpers
punished Daniel by putting him
with hungry lions. They thought the
lions would eat him. But God sent
an angel to protect Daniel.
The lions will not hurt him.

What happened to Daniel?

THIS BEAUTIFUL

woman is Queen Esther. She loves
God and is kind to God's people.
She is brave. She is telling the king
to help God's people. The king is
listening and will do what Queen
Esther has asked him to do.

What is the queen's name?

THE TEMPLE

Solomon built had been destroyed.
Now the people have built a
beautiful new Temple. It is their
church. All the people can come
and pray. God is very pleased with
his people. He wants us to go
to church and worship him.

What is this beautiful building called?

THE ANGEL GABRIEL

is telling Mary something very
important. He is telling her she
will be the mother of God's Son!
Mary is very excited! She is happy
because she will be the mother
of the Savior. She will name
the baby Jesus.

What did the angel tell Mary?

ZECHARIAH

and Elizabeth are so happy with their baby boy. An angel told Zechariah he would have a son and should name him John. When John grew up, he told people that Jesus was coming. You can tell your friends about Jesus too.

What is the baby's name?

THIS IS MARY'S

baby. Do you remember his name? It is Jesus! He is God's Son, but he was born in a barn where sheep and donkeys live. He was a great king in heaven before he came down to earth as a baby.

Where was Jesus born?

THESE SHEPHERDS

were outside taking care of their sheep. Suddenly they saw an angel. He told them Jesus had been born in a barn in the town of Bethlehem. Now many other angels have come. They are praising God because Jesus came to save us.

What did the angel tell the shepherds?

THE SHEPHERDS

ran into town to find the baby.
They found him in a barn, just as
the angel said. Mary is cuddling
her baby. Jesus looked like any baby,
but the shepherds knew he was
God's Son. The angel had told them
that Jesus is the Savior.

Where did the shepherds find Jesus?

SIMEON IS

a very old man. He has been waiting for many years to see God's Son. Mary and Joseph have brought baby Jesus to the Temple. Now Simeon is very happy! He is thanking God for this special child. His long wait is over!

Who was Simeon waiting to see?

HERE IS THE BABY

Jesus and his mother, Mary. Some wise men from far away have come with presents for Jesus. They saw a star that led them to Jesus. They know Jesus will be very great and important. That is why they are bringing him gifts.

Why are they bringing gifts to Jesus?

JOSEPH IS TAKING

Mary and the baby Jesus
on a long trip. They are running
away from some men who want
to kill the baby. They are going to
Egypt. God is taking care of Jesus
by telling Joseph to take him
far away.

Why are they taking the long trip?

JESUS AND HIS

family have returned to their home. Now Jesus is getting bigger. He is God's Son, but he is also Mary's son. He listens carefully to Mary and Joseph as they teach him. They love him, and he loves and obeys them.

Who is Jesus' mother?

JESUS HAS BECOME

a big boy. He is twelve years old.
He is in the Temple talking to the
leaders of God's people. Jesus is
listening to them and asking them
questions. They are all surprised
at his good answers.

Why are the men surprised?

JESUS HAS GROWN

up and become a man. His cousin John baptized people who loved God. John has just baptized Jesus in the river. The Holy Spirit is coming down from heaven in the form of a dove. God's voice from heaven said, "Jesus is my dear Son."

What did the voice from heaven say?

THE MAN

in the striped coat is Nicodemus.
He is asking Jesus how to get
to heaven. Jesus is telling him that
anyone who believes in God's Son
will go to heaven. Do you know the
name of God's Son? His name
is Jesus.

What is the man asking Jesus?

JESUS IS TALKING

with his friends. They are called his disciples. Some of them were fishermen, but Jesus is telling them to come with him. They will tell people that God loves them. You can tell people about Jesus, too, and that you love him.

What are Jesus' helpers called?

THIS WOMAN

came to get water from the well. Jesus told her he could give her something better than water. He could give her a happy life with God. She believed Jesus and went to tell her friends. They came and believed in Jesus too.

What could Jesus give the woman?

THESE MEN

had been fishing all night. They couldn't catch any fish. Then Jesus came and told them to try once more. He made the fish go into the net. Now the men have all these fish. Jesus is very great. He can do anything.

What did Jesus make the fish do?

JESUS IS TELLING

the people about God. He is saying
that God wants us to be kind to
everyone. He doesn't want us
to quarrel or get angry. Jesus gave
us the Golden Rule: "Do for others
what you want them to do for you."

What can you do to help someone?

THIS GIRL

was very ill. While her father was trying to find Jesus, the girl died. Jesus came to her house and said, "Get up, little girl!" And she came back to life. You can see she is well again now. What wonderful things Jesus does.

What happened to this girl?

THIS MAN

was blind. Close your eyes right
now and pretend you are blind.
Isn't it wonderful to be able to see?
"Do you believe I can make you
see?" Jesus asked the man.
"Yes," the man answered. Then
Jesus touched his eyes,
and he could see!

*What do you see when you
close your eyes?*

JESUS WAS SLEEPING

in the boat during a big storm.
His friends were scared. They
thought the boat was going to sink.
They woke Jesus up. "We are all
going to die," they screamed.
But Jesus stood up and told the
storm to go away. And it did.

What did Jesus tell the storm to do?

PETER IS

in the water. He needs help!
Jesus is coming to help him.
Jesus is not sinking like Peter
because Jesus is God's Son.
He can even walk on top of the
water! Jesus will help you, too,
if you ask him.

Could Peter walk on the water?
Could Jesus?

THE PEOPLE

were hungry. A little boy gave his lunch to Jesus. Then Jesus made it become enough for everyone. Jesus' helpers are giving the food to many, many people. Jesus can do wonderful things like that!

Who gave his lunch to Jesus?
What did Jesus do with it?

THIS WOMAN

is giving all the money she has to God's house. She is thankful for everything God has given her. She loves God and knows he will take care of her. God wants us to be thankful for all he has given us.

What can you thank God for giving you?

JESUS LOVES

children. Once some mothers
brought their children to Jesus.
Jesus' friends told them to go away.
Jesus said, "No, let them come
to me." Then Jesus held the children
in his arms and loved them.
Jesus loves you, too.

What did Jesus' friends say?
What did Jesus say?

THE MAN

on the ground was badly hurt
by robbers. Several people saw him
but didn't help him. Now a man has
stopped and is putting bandages on
his cuts. The man who helped
is called the Good Samaritan.
You can be a Good Samaritan by
helping people.

What is the Good Samaritan doing?

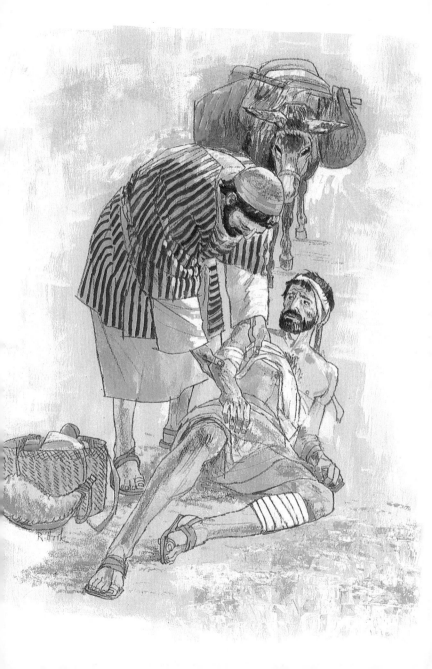

ONE DAY JESUS

ate supper with his friends
Mary and Martha. Martha was
working hard to cook dinner.
She was unhappy because Mary
was listening to Jesus. Jesus was
pleased that Mary was listening
to him. What she was doing
was very important.

Who was listening to Jesus?

A SHEPHERD

takes good care of his sheep.
He looks for them if they are lost.
He picks up the lambs if they
are hurt. Jesus said he is like
a shepherd. We are like sheep.
Even though we can't see him,
we know he takes care of us.

Who is our Good Shepherd?

LAZARUS WAS

one of Jesus' friends. He died,
and his body was wrapped up
and put into a grave in the rocks.
Jesus came and prayed. Then Jesus
shouted, "Lazarus, come out."
At once Lazarus came back to life
and came out!

What did Jesus tell Lazarus to do?

THE TEN MEN

in the picture were all very ill.
They asked Jesus to make them
well again, and he did. But only one
man came back to thank Jesus.
I hope you remember to say thank
you when someone helps you.
And always remember to say
thank you to God.

*How many of these men said
thank you to Jesus?*

THIS RICH MAN

asked Jesus how he could get to
heaven. Jesus knew the man loved
his money more than he loved God.
Jesus told him to give his money
away and give his life to God. To get
to heaven he had to love God more
than he loved his money.

What did the man love most?

LUKE 15

THIS FATHER

is hugging his son. His son ran
away and has just come home
again. He thought his father
wouldn't love him anymore!
But his father is very happy. God
is our Father in heaven, and he is
happy when we come to him.

Who is your Father in heaven?

ZACCHAEUS CLIMBED

a tree to see Jesus. Now Jesus is talking to him. Jesus is telling him, "Come down because I am going to your house today." Zacchaeus is very glad about this. Are you glad that Jesus has come to your house?

What did Jesus tell Zacchaeus?

JESUS IS COMING

into Jerusalem riding on a donkey.
The little girl is singing about how
wonderful Jesus is. The fathers and
mothers are waving branches
to show that they are happy too.
They all want Jesus to be
their new king.

What is the girl doing?

JESUS IS WASHING

the feet of one of his friends.
Usually big people wash their own
feet. They don't like to wash other
people's feet. But we should help
other people, even when we
don't want to.

*Can you think of a time when you
wanted to play, but you helped
your mother instead?*

JESUS IS EATING

supper with his good friends
for the last time. This is called the
Last Supper. He has told his friends
that soon Judas will bring the
soldiers to take him away. Then he
will be killed. Jesus died so he
can be our Savior

Who will take Jesus away?

JESUS IS PRAYING.

He knows he will soon die for our sins. He is asking God to help him. He is willing to die if that is what God wants. You and I should be like Jesus. We should always want to do what God wants us to do.

What is Jesus doing?

NOW SOMETHING

very sad is happening. Judas
and the soldiers have come
to get Jesus and take him away.
All of Jesus' friends ran away
because they were afraid.
They didn't try to help him.

What did Jesus' friends do?

PETER IS ONE

of Jesus' friends who ran away
when the soldiers came. Now Peter
is telling a lie. He says he doesn't
know Jesus. He is afraid the people
might hurt him for being Jesus'
friend. Don't ever be afraid to tell
people you love Jesus.

Why did Peter tell a lie?

THE SOLDIERS

have brought Jesus to a man named Pilate. Pilate can tell them to let Jesus go. But Pilate is afraid to say it. He is afraid people won't like him if he lets Jesus go. So he says, "Jesus must die."

Why was Pilate afraid to let Jesus go?

THEY ARE KILLING

Jesus. He is dying on a cross. Why are they killing him? Has he done anything wrong? No! He is dying because of the wrong things you and I have done. Jesus is letting God punish him because of our sins.

Why did Jesus die?

AFTER JESUS DIED,

his friends put his body
into a grave. Now it is Easter
morning. Two women are looking
into the grave. But Jesus' body isn't
there! God brought Jesus back
to life again, and he came out!
Jesus is alive again!

Is Jesus still in the grave?

AFTER JESUS

came back to life, he talked to these friends. But they didn't know it was Jesus! They were very sad because they thought Jesus was dead. Suddenly they knew he was Jesus! How happy they were to know Jesus had come back to life again!

Why were Jesus' friends sad?

LOOK WHAT IS

happening! Jesus is rising into the sky! He is going back to heaven where his Father is! He is telling his friends good-bye. But he says he will come back again. Then they will always be with him. We will be with him too.

Where is Jesus going?

A FEW WEEKS

after Jesus went back up to heaven,
he sent the Holy Spirit to live in our
hearts. Jesus' friends were
all together. Suddenly they saw
little flames on each other's heads.
Can you point to them? Then
the people began talking in other
languages they hadn't learned!

What was on their heads?

THIS MAN

had never been able to walk. Even when he was a little boy he couldn't walk. But now you can see him jumping for joy. What has happened? Jesus' friends, Peter and John, told his sickness to go away! The Holy Spirit gave them this power.

What did Peter and John do?

THE MAN KNEELING

on the grass is Stephen. He told everyone that only Jesus could forgive their sins. He wouldn't stop telling people how wonderful Jesus is. This made the people angry. They threw rocks at him until he died and went to heaven to be with Jesus.

Why were the people angry?

GOD SENT

his friend Philip to talk to
the man in the chariot. Philip is
telling the man about God. The man
wants to be God's friend. Philip is
saying he can be God's friend if he
believes in Jesus. You can be
God's friend too.

What did Philip tell the man?

PAUL WAS AN ENEMY

of Jesus. He was going to hurt and
kill people who believed in Jesus.
Suddenly there was a bright flash
of light and Paul fell down. Jesus
talked to him from heaven. After
that Paul told everyone that
Jesus is God's Son.

Who talked to Paul from heaven?

PETER IS IN JAIL

for telling people that Jesus loves
them and died for them. God has
sent an angel to help Peter. The
angel made the chains on Peter's
hands and feet fall off! The doors
of the jail were locked, but the angel
opened them without a key,
and Peter walked out.

What happened to Peter's chains?

TIMOTHY'S

grandmother is reading him
a Bible story. When he grows up
he will tell lots of people about the
Bible and about Jesus. The Bible is
the book God gave to us. It tells us
that God loves us very much.

Do you have a Bible of your own?

DO YOU REMEMBER

Paul? Now he is God's friend. He is leaving on a long trip in this ship. He is going to another country. He will tell people that Jesus loves them. Paul was a missionary. Perhaps you will be a missionary someday.

Where is Paul going?

PAUL AND SILAS

are in jail. They are in jail because they told everyone about Jesus. But God rescued his friends. He sent a great earthquake, and their chains fell off. The doors of the jail were locked, but they flew open!

How did God rescue Paul and Silas?

PAUL WAS ON A BOAT

in a great storm. The boat sank,
but God kept Paul and everyone
else safe. They all swam to land.
God didn't want Paul to die yet
because he wanted him to be a
missionary. God wanted him to tell
everyone about Jesus.

What happened to the boat?

PAUL IS IN JAIL

again. He has been there a long, long time. This time God did not send an earthquake to get him out. God still loved him just as much as ever, but he didn't rescue him. Sometimes God lets us have troubles too. But he loves us all the time.

Where is Paul?

ONE OF JESUS'

closest friends was John. When John was an old man, he had a long vision, or dream, about heaven. In his vision he saw Jesus in heaven. John wrote about what he saw. His book is called The Revelation.
It is in the Bible.

Who saw heaven in a vision?

About the Author

KENNETH N. TAYLOR is best known as the translator of *The Living Bible*, but his first renown was as a writer of children's books. Ken and his wife, Margaret, had ten children, and his early books were written for use in the family's daily devotions. The manuscripts were ready for publication only when they passed the scrutiny of those ten young critics! Those books, which have now been read to three generations of children around the world, include *The Bible in Pictures for Little Eyes* (Moody Publishers), *Devotions for the Children's Hour* (Moody Publishers), *The Living Bible Story Book* (Tyndale House), and *Big Thoughts for Little People* (Tyndale House). Now the Taylor children are all grown up, so *My First Bible in Pictures* was written with the numerous grandchildren in mind.

About the Illustrators

RICHARD and **FRANCES HOOK** have produced some of the most beloved illustrations of Bible stories. Their style became a standard for other contemporary illustrators. The Hooks worked together as a team, Richard illustrating the men and the backdrops, Frances the women and children.

The Hooks illustrated scores of Bible stories during their lifetimes. Tyndale House made arrangements with Concordia and Standard to reprint some of their Hook art in this book, but no Hook illustrations were available for some of the stories included in *My First Bible in Pictures*. To fill in the gaps, Tyndale House commissioned three illustrators to produce the remaining illustrations in a style reminiscent of Richard and Frances Hook's work.